A NOTE TO PARENTS

This story has long been a favorite with children, primarily because they enjoy reading about animals. This version emphasizes the care and love that Noah and his family gave to animals, and tells how Noah followed God's instruction to build a large boat and help his family and the animals ride out the storm. Because young children have a limited ability to think abstractly, the story does not dwell on abstract concepts of wickedness or judgement.

As you read this book, you might remind your children of times that you care for animals too. Use the book again and again as you enjoy animals, as you watch the rain on the windowpane, and as you experience a rainbow.　　　　— *Delia Halverson*

Delia Halverson is the consultant for *Family Time Bible Stories*. An interdenominational lecturer on religious education, she has written seven books, including *How Do Our Children Grow?*

Scripture sources: **Genesis 6:9 through 9:17**

FAMILY TIME
BIBLE
STORIES

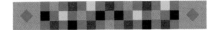

NOAH'S ARK

Retold by Patricia Daniels

Illustrated by Kathy Rusynyk

TIME
LIFE Kids™

ALEXANDRIA, VIRGINIA

Many years ago, in a faraway land, there lived a wise old farmer named Noah. Noah was a good man, and he and his family lived a peaceful life. They grew grapes and figs in the warmth of the sun and took care of their animals with gentle hands.

One day, when Noah
was tending his trees,
he heard the voice
of God.

"Noah," said God,
"a great flood is
coming. I want
you to build a huge
boat, an ark. Then
bring onto the ark
two of every kind of
animal in the world.
Your family and these
creatures will be safe
from the flood."

Noah did what God asked. From all around the land he
brought in stacks of sweet-smelling cypress wood.

Day after day, he and his sons, Shem, Ham, and Japheth, hammered and nailed the planks of the ark.

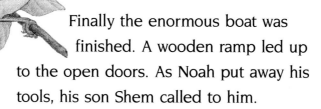

Finally the enormous boat was
finished. A wooden ramp led up
to the open doors. As Noah put away his
tools, his son Shem called to him.

"Father," he cried, "look out there!"

Noah turned around. Down every
road, over every hill, animals big and
small appeared. Birds filled the air.
Ants and ladybugs and spiders scurried
along the ground.

With a rumble of footsteps and a rush of wings the animals entered the ark. Elephants stomped up the steep ramp. Jack rabbits leaped. Swallows swooped overhead. Noah's family watched while a male and female of every animal on earth found a place aboard the ark.

The inside of the ark was busy as animals settled in on beds of straw.

Noah felt a light touch on his shoulder. It was a shy white dove, leaning close to him. "Don't worry, little one," he said, stroking its neck. Then he raised his head to listen. The first drops of rain were rattling against the side of the ark.

It rained and rained and rained. Water lifted the ark from the ground. Floating on the flood, the ark rose above

the trees. Then it rose above the highest
mountains. The rain fell for 40 days and 40 nights.

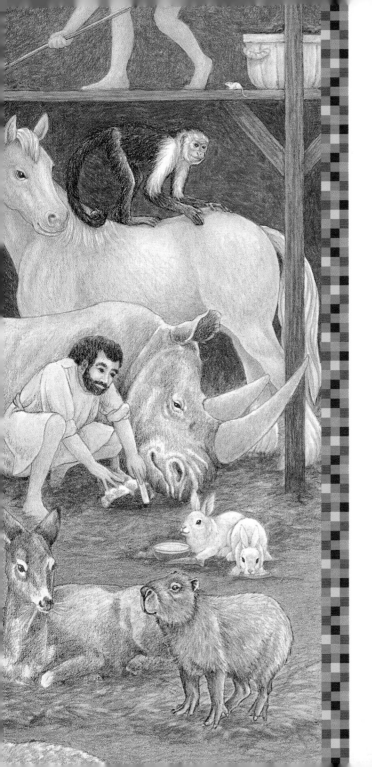

The animals felt safe inside the ark as it rode the waters. Noah's family fed and bathed them. Shem scratched the pigs' backs when they were itchy. Japheth filed the rhinos' toenails when they got too long. The little dove went everywhere on Noah's shoulder.

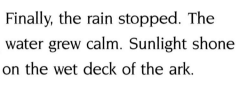

Finally, the rain stopped. The
water grew calm. Sunlight shone
on the wet deck of the ark.

Noah opened a window. "Go,
little friend," he said to the
dove. "Fly away and look for land."

The dove returned hours later, tired
and sad. Noah let it rest for a week.
Then he sent it out again. This time the
dove came back joyfully, with an olive
leaf in its beak.

"Land!" cried Noah. "Bless you,
small one!"

As the water began to drain away, Noah saw that the ark was resting on the side of a mountain. Trees and fields appeared below them. When the land was dry, Noah

opened the ark's wide doors. In pairs and in families,
the animals left the boat. They ran and flew and slithered
into the sunny valley below.

A glorious rainbow swept across the sky above the ark. God spoke again to Noah.

"This rainbow is a sign," God said. "I promise that a flood will never again cover the whole earth."

And Noah and his family and two free-flying doves settled down in the valley. They lived happily afterward through rain and shine.

TIME-LIFE KIDS®
Staff for FAMILY TIME BIBLE STORIES

Managing Editor:	Patricia Daniels
Art Director:	Susan K. White
Publishing Associate:	Marike van der Veen
Editorial Assistant:	Mary M. Saxton
Copy Editor:	Colette Stockum
Production Manager:	Marlene Zack
Quality Assurance Manager:	Miriam Newton

First printing. Printed in U.S.A. Published simultaneously in Canada.

Time Life Inc. is a wholly owned subsidiary of THE TIME INC. BOOK COMPANY.

TIME-LIFE is a trademark of Time Warner Inc. U.S.A.
School and library distribution by Time-Life Education,
P.O. Box 85026, Richmond, VA 23285-5026.
For subscription information, call 1-800-621-7026.

Library of Congress Cataloging-in-Publication Data

Daniels, Patricia, 1955- Noah's Ark / retold by Patricia Daniels; illustrated by Kathy Rusynyk. p. cm. — (Family time Bible stories)
Summary: A simple retelling of the Bible story in which Noah builds an ark and saves two of each kind of animal from the great flood. ISBN 0-7835-4626-2 1. Noah's ark — Juvenile literature. 2. Bible stories, English — O.T. Genesis. [1. Noah (Biblical figure) 2. Noah's ark. 3. Bible stories — O.T.] I. Rusynyk, Kathy, ill. II. Title. III. Series.
BS658.D29 1995   95-36897
222'.1109505 — dc20   CIP
                                                  AC